THE POWER OF NU

KARMIC DEBT 13/4

The Complete Guide

FELICIA BENDER, PHD

COPYRIGHT NOTICE

FAB Enterprises Ltd./Felicia Bender

www.feliciabender.com

ISBN Paperback: 978-0-9851682-3-0

ISBN Ebook: 978-0-9851682-5-4

CONTENTS

WELCOME TO THE WORLD OF KARMIC DEBT NUMBERS!

If a number 13 shows up anywhere in your core numerology profile as the Life Path, Expression or Destiny, Soul Urge, Birth Day, Personality or Maturity number, you've come to the right place! Also know that the Karmic Debt number can show up within a cycle of time (and other places!) within your numerology profile.

Just the name "Karmic Debt" brings up lot of feelings, right? It doesn't sound like something any of us would *like* to have in our numerology profile! Yet let's be clear. *Karma* applies to all of us, whether or not we have a Karmic Debt number as part of our numerology. *Karma* itself is neutral. It's the law of "cause and effect." If you drop an egg on the floor, it will crack. If you drive your car without filling it up with gas (or electricity), it will stop moving. Is a broken egg "bad?" Is it a *punishment* to you if you're stranded without an operating vehicle? No, it's simply the result of an action or an inaction.

If you see a Karmic Debt number in your chart, this does not mean you're bad or being punished! It also doesn't mean that you'll have a really awful or hard life. What it *does* mean is that you'll have some added layers of "drivers" in your life that can become easier to handle when you actually know what they are!

A client of mine who has a Karmic Debt Life Path number expressed to me that he considers his Karmic Debt to be a Karmic *gift*! That's the way we will approach this as we move through the explanation about how to comprehend and use the information the Karmic Debt number brings to our lives.

Before we begin our journey describing and understanding the nature of the Karmic Debt number 13/4, let's do a quick review of the origin of numerology so that you can understand the specific type of numerology we're using to define the Karmic Debt 13/4.

Since you're reading this book, I've made an assumption that you're already familiar with your numerology enough to be intrigued to know more about the Karmic Debt number 13/4. I've chosen not to map out all the calculations and explanations for each number in a numerology profile in this guide. If you want to go into depth with your numerology profile, please reference my book *The Ultimate Guide To Practical Numerology: Mapping Your Path & Purpose.* You can also order a numerology profile at http://FeliciaBender.com or find numerology profiles through various on-line resources. With that said, let's get started dissecting the Karmic Debt 13/4!

WHAT IS NUMEROLOGY, ANYWAY?

What *is* numerology?

For clarity, there are different kinds of numerology, just like there are different forms of astrology and different forms of any "olgy." I'm working with Pythagorean numerology and this is the type of numerology you'll learn in this guide.

Numerology was developed around 530 b.c.e. by Pythagoras, a Greek mathematician, philosopher, and mystic—remember the Pythagorean Theorem of Geometry? *Same guy.* Pythagoras suggests that each number not only represents a quantity (for instance, one apple, two apples, and so on), it also carries a *vibration and a frequency* that has a particular meaning and influence.

Much like gravity or the mystery of cell phone reception, we don't have to understand how it affects us or even to believe in it for it to operate. It's rather like Morse Code. To the untrained, hearing the random dots and dashes of Morse Code just seems like random or garbled sounds. Yet to those trained in the language of Morse Code, the dots and dashes communicate very specific information. You just have to know the language to understand it.

It's the same with numerology. Once you learn the defining qualities of the numbers 1-9—along with some additional "code"—you can understand the message and information that the numbers carry with them whenever they show up. Some numbers have some deeper meaning and carry some added elements to the game when they show up, like Karmic Debt numbers or Master numbers. The Karmic Debt numbers are 13/4, 14/5, 16/7 and 19/1. Master numbers are the repeating numbers 11/2, 22/4, and 33/6.

If numerology resonates with you, digging deeper into the meaning of these special numbers offers a reservoir of knowledge, information, and answers. In this guide, we're focusing on the key elements of the Karmic Debt number 13/4.

KARMIC DEBT

The Karmic Debt number 13/4 indicates that you have to "balance the scales" in this lifetime for the actions performed in a former lifetime. Of course, this is based in a belief in reincarnation—that our souls incarnate from lifetime to lifetime in order to have certain experiences and learn specific lessons. When a Karmic Debt number shows up, it's revealing to you that you'll experience significant challenges with a particular "topic" in your life. It depends on where it lands in your chart as to what the over-all effect might be.

Understand also that your chart consists of many numbers and influence, so if you have the Karmic Debt 13/4, it'll play a part in your overall personality and yet it isn't the only factor. I can't emphasize this enough: You're not bad. You're not being punished. You're simply paying back a debt and working in an additional way to balance your *Karma*. Everyone has *Karma* to balance. Everyone is working through Karmic elements in their lives!

The concept of Karmic Debt in numerology is dependent upon the notion of reincarnation and past lives. The origin of how we have come to view reincarnation apparently originated in India sometime near 800 B.C. Reincarnation is a "given" as a foundational belief in Buddhism and Hinduism.

Reincarnation is the belief that the soul never dies, it simply passes through a succession of lives. The soul is eternal and continues to incarnate into different bodies in different lifetimes in order to gain certain experience and to learn particular lessons. The concept of *Karma* is associated with reincarnation. *Karma* is essentially the law of cause and effect. *Karma* is the direct result (from lifetime-to-lifetime) of the deeds (positive or negative) of one's past lives. Further, it's believed that these events and actions from past manifestations affect this present life. To extend this belief, the Law of Karma also tells us that our present deeds and experiences will have ramifications for future lives as our soul incarnates again.

The great thing about having basic knowledge about where your particular Karmic Debt is located gives you a great advantage as you make efforts to understand some of the difficulties you experience and also why you might have certain feelings and underlying issues with particular areas of your life.

In this guidebook, we'll dig into the nitty-gritty and deconstruct the Karmic Debt 13/4 in order to reveal the nuances that this energy brings to your life. We'll focus on the opportunities it offers as well as the challenges to be mastered and integrated into your experience.

We'll go over the qualities of the number 4, because that is the foundational point of purpose and the task for you if you have the 13/4 in your numerology profile. Yet it's invaluable to also look at the numbers 1 and 3, because this is what you're also being called upon to pull into your thoughts, feelings, and actions when you're engaging with the 13/4. I'll explain this more directly as we go along. The purpose is to empower and provide some cheerleading for you as you work to understand what's required in order to do well on your 13/4 Karmic Debt test!

And remember this: If you're taking enough interest in your life and in your personal growth to actually seek out this information, chances are you're on the upside of working through your Karmic Debt. People who are still enmeshed in the same behaviors that earned them the debt in the first place are rarely seeking out support and metaphysical solutions.

I'm excited to share some insights into the 13/4 and share some resources, ideas, and overall support for you as you navigate what you've come here to do. As we go through this guide, it's meant to show you how to begin to understand the layers and the nuance that the 13 brings to the energy and demands of the Karmic 13/4.

Be aware that most often you'll consider the 13/4 *just a 4*. Only when you get into more depth with numerology do you start being able to handle the deeper meaning and deeper information these significant numbers bring to your life. First, we'll go over the key characteristics of the number 4. After all, this is the foundational element of the Karmic 13/4, so we need to have our bearings around the optimal qualities of the 4 before we dig deeper into the 13.

THE MESSAGE OF THE 13/4

If you have a 13/4 as one of your core numbers, understand that you're now paying back for past life abuses where carrying your share of the workload and your share of personal responsibility was seriously abused.

The number 1 in 13 indicates *selfishness* in a past life. A heightened level of selfishness is the common denominator for all of the Karmic Debt numbers. Then we look to see what number is standing next to the 1 for a clue as to what category the selfish behavior was enacted. In this case, there was selfishness within the elements of the number 3—communication, expression, optimism, and joy. With this Karmic Debt number, you're being called upon to balance your *Karma* by aligning with the highest and best of the hardworking, responsible, and systematic 4 *while also engaging positively with the optimal characteristics of the playful and creative 3.*

The Karmic Debt 13/4 indicates that in a past life you were lazy, superficial, and didn't take personal responsibility for your actions (or inactions). You got to play the ultimate victim, blaming everyone else for your lack of success, resources or motivation. On top of that, you also expressed negatively through sarcasm, pessimism, and cutting people down with words. The number 3 in the Karmic Debt 13/4 represents creative energy, expression, and joyfulness that turned into superficiality, irresponsibility, and using words to hurt others.

As a Karmic Debt number, the 13 indicates that putting the petal-to-the-metal and digging in with some hard work and ongoing effort will be an ongoing requirement in this lifetime. The 13/4 tells you that you're being asked to monitor and master the *art of positive expression*—and you can understand that as thinking before you speak, not being critical and judgmental, and using your words to support and uplift others rather than to tear them down.

I also say that the key element to the 13/4 Karmic Debt is to learn to whistle while you work! You'll always be the one carrying a bit more of the workload, so why not make the most of it? You're also required to develop a strong sense of discipline and use responsible action in all practical matters. The 13/4 often gravitates toward teaching on some level, yet with a performative flair! There is a talent for creative expression and yet with this Karmic Debt, that talent might take a while to trust or to develop. There can be substantial blockages with emotional expression and with self-expression. Yet you'll always be given opportunities to grow into these attributes, move through self-doubt, and make good use of your creative talents.

4 | THE BASICS

The 4 is what you're being asked to engage on its highest and best levels. It's as though you're being called to become the poster child for the best elements of this hard-working and pragmatic energy. It's valuable to understand the best qualities of the number 4 so that you can be intentional about aligning yourself with those traits. Yet it's also extremely valuable to know the opposing forces at work. There will always be heightened challenges to be worked with and with the Karmic Debt, these can feel a bit more intense. There are the "over-active" and the "under-active" aspects of the 4 to be grappled with and worked through.

The 4 is connected with: material interests, structure, managing finances, creating lasting foundations, hard work, stable finances, solid management, organization, efficiency, physical activity, physical health, limitations.

Optimal: dependable, reliable, thrifty, methodical, analytical, productive, solid, cautious, disciplined, sensible, loyal, trustworthy, and persevering.

Over-active: rigid, narrow minded, worrisome, inflexible, dreary, emotionally overwhelmed, uncompromising, small-minded, blunt, and lost in (or over-focused on) details.

Under-active: disorganized, apathetic, sarcastic, impractical, careless, inefficient, distracted, idle, self-absorbed, uncentered, and neglectful.

Process and Stability

The 4 is all about developing stability through process. The 4 is cerebral, intelligent, and a seeker and cultivator of knowledge. If you were to audition for the cast of *Winnie the Pooh*, you would land the role of Owl—really smart, if not slightly smug and bossy.

Because the 4 knows how to build solid foundations, you're often placed in charge of developing operating systems and are expected to look after the details. You're the workhorse and "master builder" of the world. The 4 devours information so that when you find a topic or subject that interests you, there's no end to the depth of your knowledge about it and your ability to impart that knowledge to others.

You're a born teacher. You may not become a teacher in the traditional sense, yet you demonstrate an undeniable depth of knowledge and just can't help sharing what you know with others. Your mission in life is to learn the advantages of using system and order. You're learning and mastering how to use system, order, and effort to your benefit and to the benefit of others.

You'll be tempted to skip steps on the way—yet when you do, you'll have to go "back to go" (for Monopoly fans: "Don't pass go, don't collect $200"). You're becoming a master of step-by-step processes. Yet understand that this might not be your preferred comfort zone! This is something you must work at cultivating and mastering throughout your life. You manifest great things when you articulate a goal and then map out all the steps it will take to get there. The 4's learning to be method-ical, reliable, and success comes to you when you commit to practical and realistic outcomes.

Someone wrote this comment about the 4 on my YouTube channel: "4 is boring!" I would argue with that on various lev-els. Just not so! Jimmy Fallon has a 4 Life Path—Tina Fey, Brad Pitt, Quinton Tarantino, Oprah Winfrey, Keanu Reeves, and others are 4s. Are these folks boring? *Au contraire*! These are just some celebrity examples (see more well-known 13/4's listed at the end of this guide). The point to be made is this. The 4 is in it (whatever "it" is) for the *long-haul*. There's nothing that the 4 can't manifest, yet it comes with deep roots and a solid foundation.

Hard Work

The 4 is the number of hard work and concerted effort. With a 4, your "lucky breaks" are few and far between. Whatever you do requires effort, fortitude, and tenacity. It's rare that you'll find yourself in the mist of something that doesn't require you to put in the hours (overtime, anyone?) to get it done.

While others are frolicking at the coffee shop behind their computer screens, more than likely you're on your feet behind the counter, out in the "field," training or any number of other more down-to-earth activities. It's funny about the 4, because sometimes you'll find yourself—in your younger years—considerably less directed, if not confused about your path in life in terms of determining the work or career that might light you up.

You can squeak by in school without much effort (you're a smartie, after all!), be totally non-directed about a career or college major, take odd physical jobs or low-paying jobs, sit around smoking pot on the couch, and whatever other diversions you can concoct. Yet as time wears on, you'll feel this gnawing sense of unrealized purpose and potential that will keep hounding you until you make the leap and decide to focus on something, step it up, get some systems and routines in order, show up to the table, and make an effort.

It's all about taking responsibility for your life—and when you turn this corner, it starts to feel really gratifying. And often this "Eureka!" moment happens when you truly see that when you (and only you) are responsible for yourself and aren't frustrated or depressed that there isn't someone swooping in like a

Knight in Shining Armor to save or support you. On the other end of the spectrum, that "Eureka!" moment can also happen when we decide not to feel an overburdened sense of responsibility for other people. *Easier said than done, right 4?*

You can be that 4 who grows up in the trenches, working at an early age, and taking on more adult responsibilities for your own well-being than a "normal" child. You can be the one who works his or her way through school while forgoing the traditional college partying and socializing. You must be serious about your finances—because they're sparse and you receive little to no support otherwise and so you miss out on the lighter or more fun elements of life out of this financial necessity. In this way, you can become the "realist" fairly early in life. Often the 4 spends most of their lives seeking a basic level of foundational support and security that they never had (or never felt they had) as a child.

You can also *choose* to do more "serious" endeavors as opposed to engaging in the more frivolous aspects of life when growing up—or even in adult life. It's as though you don't have time, energy or desire to engage in activities that aren't designed to *get you somewhere.* You tend to be immensely pragmatic and logical. Either way, "hard work" is a consistent theme for you and you're learning—while you will always exert more than the lion's share of work—how to modulate it by either not being a work martyr or a slacker.

Systems and Foundations

The 4 feels most comfortable when moving slowly and deliberately. You work out your plan and want life to be orderly.

Underneath all that planning is a fear of chaos and a real dislike of appearing stupid or naïve in any situation. Overall, you're eminently practical, hardworking, and determined. No matter what, you'll get it done. No doubt about it, you're the rock!

Think about the how the number 4 looks when drawn on a piece of paper. If you turn the 4 upside-down it resembles a chair—a sturdy surface planted solidly on the ground. It can also resemble a box with four-corners. And everyone knows that the 4 has a tendency to stay inside the box, so to speak. With a 4 you're meant to contribute the foundational ideas, products, services or systems of management to the world. *You bring matter into material form.*

The 4 is "earth" energy and thrives when connected with the earth in a variety of ways—whether literally in the garden with your hands and feet in the dirt—or more broadly through your gifts having to do with planning and making sure the foundations are securely set. The 4 is known as the "architect" number and often gravitates toward building or construction on some level.

Knowledge

With a 4, you're always absorbing information and seeking out knowledge. As an example: when a family member is diagnosed with cancer, you immediately research everything there is to know about that particular form of cancer, consolidate the information, share it with other family members, and wonder why everyone else doesn't actively do the same.

Animals often play an important role in your life, either as pets/family members or—in the wider sense—a 4 will often be found in the position of President of the Audubon Society, Humane Society or other animal-related organization or cause.

And while you have plenty of creativity, often it displays in more technical ways—photography, calligraphy, musical instruments—anything that calls for technical skill rather than flamboyant creativity.

Overall, you're often the bookworm and the one who pays for the documentary channel. You're the one who'll learn everything there is to know about a particular country or city if you're planning to travel there. The 4's the one who actually balances your checkbook, has money in your savings account (yet if you don't, you're miserable about it), and enjoys a few interesting hobbies—like cheese-making, car renovation or raising chickens.

Slow and Steady

Because of a potentially volatile past, you have a desire to *protect*—yourself, things, and the people around you. You like things that are tangible and solid. Honesty and loyalty are crucial to you. You take in everything and experience a lot of sensory over-load—meaning, you are best when doing one thing at a time, not multitasking. You process information with a slower and steadier pace. Anytime you feel pressed to think more quickly or juggle several tasks at once, it can lead to feelings of overwhelm.

The 4 is a literal thinker. *Yes or No. Right or Wrong. This or That. Black or White.* You're learning how to integrate actual emotions into your existence and to grasp emotional nuances within relationship communication. It's not that you don't *have* emotions. It's just that they don't serve much of a function and so it's much easier to detach from that aspect of life and stick with things that are doable, quantifiable, and actionable.

Because you absorb and process information with great depth, you need to take plenty of time for yourself and culti-vate peace and quiet in your environment. This is imperative for your mental and physical health. You have a sensible, tra-ditional, well-behaved way about you and aren't "into" peo-ple who are otherwise. You don't understand people who are big risk takers, don't follow the rules or don't thrive in a more structured work or family environment. You sometimes have a "loner" quality to you. The 4 usually has no issues with spend-ing time alone.

Work and Career

Since "hard work" is a theme for the energy of the number 4, you might find yourself in one of two camps—either you have always taken on much more responsibility than most people or you avoid taking on responsibility and putting down roots.

My favorite quote from a 4: "That's why it's called *work*. It's not *supposed* to be *fun*." And since "work" is a constant theme, many 4s have some difficulty connecting with the job or career that truly lights them up. It often takes a while for a 4 to get clear on what they want to do given that "work" ultimately defines how you truly identify yourself in the world. A 4 who doesn't settle on a favorable career or a home base ultimately feels like a soul lost at sea. You need to plant roots and build a solid life for yourself.

The 4 is the "architect" number and you often thrive in the construction industry. Anything requiring effort and endurance works well for you, including being an athlete, any construction trade, landscaping, law enforcement or military. Teaching in any capacity is a great fit for the 4. You do well in management positions and thrive with prescribed rules and regulations—and you prefer a fair and equitable salary with clear rewards and a benefit program. You would forgo a little more money (and more volatility) for less money (and more consistency and predictability).

In Relationship

In relationship, you're solid, steady, and no-nonsense. If you're a woman, you may be strong to the point of being perceived as more "masculine" because of your "take charge" energy—you take care of everything and are super responsible.

Many (not all!) 4 women are drawn to intimate relationships with a partner whom they end up financially supporting. If you're a 4 man, you don't want drama—you want a partner who appreciates your ability to provide a secure and safe haven. You're not one to embrace a lot of change or volatility in relationship.

And as a 4, the first cut is the deepest (as Rod Stewart would say) and you can often carry-over your emotional wounds from the first divorce (or first rejection) in a way that rivals no other. It becomes the baseline for all your reaction and engagement in other relationships, often to your detriment. And at the risk of looking gullible or wrong, you can either trip from similar relationship to similar relationship or opt for staying on the fence.

Either way, opening yourself to a certain level of vulnerability can prove to be a challenge. You can often put on the front that you've "gotten over" all of it (your alcoholic ex, your abusive father, your absent mother) and *intellectually*, that may be true. Often you take the more stoic route (or the "holier-than-thou" route) and distance yourself from your emotional trauma. Yet you're always going to be asked to come back to it, acknowledge it, and do what it takes to heal it.

You can be the person who's self-depreciating about the difficulties you've had, downplaying it under the guise of: "Other people have had a far harder than I have. I don't have anything to complain about." While it can be positive not to allow your difficulties to define you or limit you, one of the lessons is located in your ability to understand and see your trauma as *your trauma*. It's yours and guides and effects your life. The power of it can't be trivialized or placed inside of a hermetically sealed box.

On a core emotional level, working through these difficult and complex family issues is key to your life's work and also key to forming a life with someone with whom you can feel safe and secure. And doing this isn't something that truly has a finish point—it's an ongoing and life long process.

4 | POSSIBLE CHALLENGES

It's Just Not Funny

While the 4 can certainly have a sense of humor and moments of lightheartedness, you tip the scales toward seriousness, brainy activity, and rational thought. Sometimes your opinions and assertions have a tendency to land like a sledgehammer. The 4 may come off as cynical or patronizing when you offer advice, yet what you're really trying to do is offer information you think will help a person or a situation.

Some might observe that the 4 can have a certain smug quality. You're most often a "literal" thinker rather than an emotions-based thinker. You're the first to say you don't want to argue and yet you most often end up in arguments because the 4 tends to be opinionated about things you feel you know a lot about. You need a lot of positive affirmation and are uncomfortable with, or even afraid of, criticism. If you can't do something perfectly according to your standards, you often don't do it at all.

As a result, sometimes you wonder why you feel so stuck or why nothing ever "works out" for you. The 4 can make the same mistake over and over (and over) again—the irony being that your primary goal is *not* to *ever* make a mistake, let alone repeat a mistake. This can show up as repeating patterns of behaviors that are self-limiting.

For instance, a friend of mine is a 4 Life Path and had a tendency to jump in to "save" her family members. She would take on financial burdens that were to help her brother, mother, father or other relative, yet the person she was "saving" would simply go about their business doing the same things that got them into dire straits to begin with—leaving her with massive debt and without a positive outcome or even a shard of appreciation or acknowledgement for her sacrifices. She would pay her brother's back rent and give him $5,000 to get himself back on track after his messy divorce, only to have him spend the money on frivolous things, landing him right back into the situation she attempted to bail him out of. She didn't have a lot of money and would go into credit card debt to assist her family and then would become enraged that she was left in debt and that they'd taken advance of her.

Limitation

The number 4 is about *limitation*. You're here to learn how to identify how you limit yourself and also how to move through (around or over) the limitations presented to you. Given that this is a "theme" for the vibe of the 4, you'll get more than your share of limitations in your life. The 4 is known for being more of an "inside the box" thinker and you benefit from allowing yourself to rise above the water line— so to speak—and see that there are other ways of thinking and operating. Often the 4 is the ultimate micromanager and only when you step out of your own way can you truly have success. Learning to be flexible and to take responsibility for yourself is the key to working with the energy of the 4. A key to this lesson is to truly see how the 4 can often create their own "prison" and then constantly feel as though they are a victim of unfair or harsh circumstances.

Just one example might be that the 4 decides to foster sick animals and yet takes on far more responsibility that is healthy for themselves (financially, time, and energy). They do this without foundational support from anyone else in their lives and then feel trapped within the responsibilities that they set up for themselves. Usually this leads to burn-out, resentment, and sometimes is an impetus for health issues.

Family Wounds or Trauma

Home is important to you. You crave a sense of security that "home" exemplifies. One of the primary issues faced by the 4 is the necessity to work through issues with family of origin. While all of us have family history to deal with, the 4 rides a particularly rough or intense road with family that's at the core of the healing and learning you've come here to do.

Many 4's have family histories that include literal or figurative abandonment, abusive parents, drug or alcohol abuse by one or both parents, an early death of a loved one, and other forms of trauma. If you're a parent of a 4, understand that this doesn't always necessarily come directly from parents. This can stem from experiences with family members, siblings, friends, teachers, and others. Some 4's experience issues that are perhaps more subliminal, yet still make a mark on you in a core way that effects how you engage with the world.

In order to work optimally with the gifts of the 4, you benefit when you take a look at wounded or problematic relationships and work through the feelings of lack and pain they've brought to you. Often this comes when you create a secure environment for yourself in whatever way works for you, either in the creation of the family you wish you'd had or mindfully choosing your "family" of choice with friends, pets, and others. Often a 4 will staunchly assert that they're "over" their family issues and yet they still occupy a lot of emotional energy. It's a matter of truly coming to terms with it and letting it go in a deep way. One of the most profound lessons for the 4 is to lighten up and take life less seriously. Not to cast off responsibilities, yet to place it all into perspective and let go of being a self-imposed manager of the universe. Of course, all human beings benefit from healing their personal trauma. It's just that this is a foundational theme for the 4 and is often a contributor to your intense need for security. Down deep, the 4 craves unconditional love that wasn't given during their foundational years.

For instance, I know a 4 young woman who's an only child and her parents divorced when she was three-years old. She went back and forth between her mother and father's houses (sometimes a three-hour drive one way) as a child. She moved to different towns (and attended different schools) frequently with her mother's job changes. While she's adaptable, she craves the stability that she didn't have as a child. And this guides her choices as she's faced with decisions about college and projecting what she wants for her future. She's a bright and intelligent young woman and yet doesn't really see the world as her oyster—rather she wants to create a world that she feels is less chaotic and unpredictable. That can become a coping mechanism for a 4 and ends up creating a more limited reality.

Rigidity

There is a definitive tendency for the 4 to develop somewhat rigid "black and white" rules for life that you feel everyone should adhere to, respect, and act upon. Let's face it—you're baffled at people who can't make a plan, who don't follow the rules, and who live more in the emotional realm. These people just need to get real, get with the program, and get a life, right?

For the 4, rigid thinking begets a rigid physical body as well. You're challenged with devoting effort to keeping your mind and body flexible. You benefit when you have friends or a partner who pushes you just a little bit out of your comfort zone and encourages you to take a little risk. Part of the result of rigidity comes out as blunt communication. And while there is something to be said for honesty, I always remember hearing actress Kristen Bell in an interview where she quoted her therapist who said: "Honesty without tact is cruelty." The 4 benefits with the cultivation of tact, diplomacy, and attempting to see others' points of view.

Let's Start Putting It Together

Now that we've outlined the basics about the number 4, let's start putting it together with the Karmic Debt 13/4. Remember that there can be complexities here that stem from different methods of calculation.

Often the 13/4 can also be calculated as the Master 22/4. It depends on your preferred method of calculation as to the final result. Meaning, in numerology there are different methods of calculation that affect the double-digit number prior to a reduction to a one-digit number.

For instance, let's take a look at Nicole Kidman's birth date and calculate her Life Path number. June 20, 1967

Method #1:

Add the Month + Day + Year

June = 6

$20 = 2 + 0 = 2$

$1967 = 1 + 9 + 6 + 7 = 23$ and $2 + 3 = 5$

$6 + 2 + 5 = 13$ and 13/4 is a Karmic Debt number

Method #2:

Add "the long way."

$6 + 2 + 0 + 1 + 9 + 6 + 7 = 31$ and $3 + 1 = 4$

With this method of calculation, Nicole Kidman doesn't have a Karmic Debt 13/4 as her Life Path number. Instead, she shows a 31/4.

What does that mean, really?

I find that it means that it's a judgment call on your part. You're the only person whose living your life experience. In my numerology practice, the month + day + year method of calculation is what I use, yet when it comes to Karmic Debt numbers (and Master numbers), I encourage looking at both methods of calculation.

It's best if you school yourself on the Master 22/4 and also the Karmic Debt 13/4. Overall, my stance is this: *You really came in to master the entirety of the essence and actionability of the number 4!*

As we look at the Karmic Debt 13/4, it's valuable to investigate the primary qualities of the 3, because the infraction in the Karmic Debt is based in this number. I find that you're being asked to infuse a lot of 3 energy into your 4, which is sometimes tricky, yet not at all impossible! Yet it helps to understand your basic job description before you head to work, if you know what I mean!

3 | THE BASICS

The 3 is what you had problems with last time around. Now you're being beckoned to master the most positive aspects of the vibrant and creative number 3 and infuse that into the highest and best version of the 4. It's valuable to understand the best qualities of the number 3 so that you can be intentional about aligning yourself with those traits. Yet it's also extremely valuable to know the opposing forces at work. There are the "over-active" and the "under-active" aspects of the 3 to be grappled with and worked through.

The 3 is connected with: pleasure, joy, optimism, self-improvement, laughter, sexual expression, artistic creativity, communication, writing, quick recoveries, easy money, instability, and dramatic emotional ups and downs.

Optimal: literary talent, cultivated, amusing, witty, well-liked, magnetic, optimistic, inspiring, authentic emotional expression, inventive, imaginative, artistic, emotionally connected, and intelligent.

Over-active: scattered, over-confident, gossipy, superficial, exaggerating, lacking concentration, difficulty with follow through, emotionally volatile, and irresponsible.

Under-active: depressed, jealous, self-doubting, inarticulate, unthinking, indecisive, bored, petty, temperamental, insincere, unenthusiastic, pessimistic, and fearful.

Performance and Expression

The 3 was born to perform and take center stage, however you personally define this. You love creativity, communication, and connecting with people. The optimal 3 communicates brilliantly and clearly, consolidating information easily. You're a master at intuitively knowing how to rework that information into new ideas. You embrace your brimming creative impulses with gusto.

Overall, the 3 can be the life of the party—clever, witty, the clown, entertaining, and good company. You make a great host or hostess and people feel nurtured and comfortable around you. You make it all look so easy. Often the 3 has many creative skills and talents in select areas, including theatre/film/

TV/broadcasting, dance, cooking, music, photography, speaking, writing or coaching/self-help. You're naturally inclined to the arts and other forms of expression that offer a conduit for your effervescent energy and unbridled creativity.

Communication

Since your life's work is all about communication, you're being asked to hone and perfect your communication skills every day and in every way. In communication, you're usually direct and compassionate, yet if you're still developing these skills, your tendency might be to become domineering and to state your thoughts and feelings bluntly, which is hard on those around you. You may end up regretting things you say, so contemplating what you want to communicate and how you want to say it—hopefully in a supportive way, with a little cushion underneath it—will be in your best interest. You can also work long and hard to even identify that you *have* feelings or opinions. If this is the case, your communication is rudimentary at best or non-existent at worst. Sometimes this miscommunication comes across as being inappropriate. Many 3's attempt to be funny and yet can come off as cringe-worthy. Oftentimes, the 3 can default into sarcasm and inappropriate humor. This is the person who's talking all the time and saying absolutely nothing.

And on the other end of the spectrum, this is the person who never communicates anything at all. They clam up and never express thoughts, opinions or emotions and then wonder why they never experience emotionally satisfying relationships. Just know that the 3 sometimes goes through periods of "stunted" communication where they can, for instance, be great communicating on the job and yet in family and personal relationships they're in their infancy. Either way, communication is a theme the 3 works with all your life.

Joy and Optimism

The 3 is truly the energy of *joie de vivre* (the joy of life). Part of your function is to appreciate and express the simple joy of living. Sounds easy, right? This is one of the many ironies of the 3, because often the 3 struggles with finding the lightness within all of the heavy emotional energy you're here to experience, process, and express.

One of the major goals for the 3 is to see and engage with the lighter elements of life and bring joy and optimism into your interactions. Ultimately, you're here to inspire and uplift others—and yet you achieve this by tapping into deep core emotional elements in your own life and in the lives of other people. The power of the 3 resides in your ability to bridge for yourself (and for others) the gap between fully experiencing all of your emotions—the good, bad and the ugly—and come through on the other side with pearls of wisdom gained through delving deeply into the emotional crevices.

And add to that, you must come out the other side with humor, good grace, and healthy discernment. You're here to learn to speak your truth, find your joy, and be creative. As you do this, your effect on others has rather glorious ramifications. As you move through life, you serve as an example to others of how to move through adversity and come out smiling—not in a saccharin or "fake" sort of way —in a real and profound way.

Emotion Ocean

If you're working the constructive aspects of the number 3, you're connected with your emotions and you have a lot of them. Many 3s spend years learning to gauge that they even *have* emotions and then they spend more years learning how to express them in a creative and healthy way. Many 3s take years to come to terms with your emotional life and the way in which you have hardwired your coping mechanisms for emotional engagement.

The 3 is intensely emotionally attuned to others (you rival the number 2 in this particular arena) and often you don't realize to what extent you pick up the emotional flotsam and jetsam from those around you—and you carry it in your overloaded backpack (metaphorically speaking) forever. Or at least until you can get a handle around what's "yours" and what's "everyone else's." You're like tofu —you take on the flavors of whatever you're soaking in.

There are 3s who choose the stoic route, not acknowledging emotions in any way, shape or form. Yet often this won't last long until there is a major health issue or other crisis that breaks the emotional center wide open. And then there are 3s who spiral out of control as they exaggerate and accentuate every fragment of their emotional engagement to the point of exasperation. The goal for the 3 is to embrace emotions, experience them, and move through them fully and completely.

Quick Wit and Intellect

The energy of the 3 is vital, curious, and quick. Your mind moves so quickly that when someone is slow thinking you easily get frustrated. Your brain moves a mile a minute and while that's a gift it can also be part of your challenge. One of the components of the 3 is the energy of creation—the 3 is the number of the Trinity, after all.

It's your birthright with a 3 to experience, dabble, and study a wide variety of "things" during your life. Yet you're also being asked to ultimately take all of that information and experience and create something unique with it. Your highest and best use is when you can settle on something (or a focused combination of things!) and bring it into practical reality.

Often a 3 can get into their 40s or beyond and experience defeat and frustration because you feel you have nothing to show for yourself. You can easily become the jack-of-all-trades and master of none. And often this happens because you feel that you'll disappoint other people if you do what you're really called to do. It's your task to step into yourself and take your talents seriously—and have fun doing it.

In fact, one of the pressures of the 3 is that you're so good at everything you do, you can have a difficult time choosing what to focus on. Often you feel that "everyone can do that!" even when no one actually can—you have a tendency to downplay your talents. Sometimes you have difficulties following through on plans. You may observe that you just can't decide how to direct your energy and become scattered and ultimately depressed and ineffective at completing whatever you set out to do. *So many ideas, so little time.*

One of the reasons is that you can talk yourself out of virtually anything and you can also become distracted or easily bored. You can find the tiniest fault with your "big idea" that stops you from proceeding past the fun part. You like fun and immediacy—you thrive during the conception phase of a project or idea. Yet when it comes down to following through and focusing on the often tedious tasks involved with getting some created and off the ground, the 3 can abandon it and move onto something else (and start the whole process over again!). Although the 3 has a great amount of reserve and tenacity, you often spend it on other people and not on yourself.

In Relationship

The 3 is passionate, energetic, and fun. You're a giver at heart and therefore you must be careful about with whom you spend your time because you'll attract "takers" if you aren't careful. You must learn to walk away from relationships unbalanced in this specific way. You're most often physically and emotionally passionate and crave relationships that are based in a deep emotional connection. You want and need a partner who's emotionally available.

One of the most basic needs for the 3 is your need to be heard. You need to have a partner who'll encourage your emotional expression—someone who will consistently listen and support you as your go through your process. *Your* job within this partnership is to discipline your emotions and not drown in your emotional life. You can be romantic and fiercely loyal.

You're a natural counselor who sees potential in others, so you might choose a partner who is a "patient" you think you can save or fix, either consciously or unconsciously.

The 3 can also find relationships too confining for their passionate spirit. Sometimes a 3 is more "married" to their creative projects than they are to another person. Or alternately, the 3 gives up their independence in relationships and squelches their creativity—or "dumbs it down" so substantially that they feel they aren't living up to their purpose in life. This is when depression becomes a regular force in the life of the 3.

Career and Work

It's not surprising to find many 3s in entertainment, politics, speaking, broadcasting, writing or any other industry that requires expert communication skills, intellect, adaptability, and a good sense of humor. Any profession where you can present your ideas to an audience is right up your alley. The key for you is to understand that you're spending a lifetime developing and honing your communication skills. Therefore, you'll have opportunity after opportunity to practice and perfect this in both your personal and professional realms.

You aren't a nine-to-five job person—you don't necessarily work well under the supervision of others or within a rigid structure. The 3 is the ultimate "up-cycler." You learn about so many different things and experience so many different things —then you sit down and take everything you're really good at and that you really love and put it all together and create something new and relevant that you can then "give out" to the world. This can be an idea, product, service—or just way of viewing and engaging with the world.

Remember, at the end of the day you're here to inspire and uplift both yourself and others—and that can take on many different qualities and manifestations. I don't know one 3 whose had a linear "resumé." The 3 usually has various degrees (or trainings/certifications) and if they don't, their life experience makes up for it. At the end of the day, the 3 often has many jobs, many certifications, and many career paths. You're most satisfied when you're able to use your creativity while inspiring and motivating others.

3 | POSSIBLE CHALLENGES

Self-Doubt and Fear of Criticism

One of the biggest obstacles for the 3 is intense self-doubt. Feelings of insecurity can stop you in your tracks and literally stun you into submission. While everyone experiences self-doubt at certain times in life, this is a ruling factor with the 3. Fear of criticism hits a 3 very hard, particularly in the younger years. So much so that a 3 will often abandon or sublimate their creative track because of a not-so-supportive experience. Avoid getting stuck overanalyzing or over thinking every single thing. You'll mud wrestle with "analysis paralysis" over and over again. When you resort to that, you'll drive yourself—and everyone else—crazy. When you experience these feelings, your best action is to *take action*, even when you feel paralyzed. Just moving through the doubt by taking *one step beyond it* will turn what used to be your biggest enemy into your personal house pet.

Especially early on, the fear of criticism is overwhelming. I have worked with 3s who were told by drunk Uncle Charlie when they were twelve-years old that being an actor was stupid. And despite the fact that being an actor was the only thing they ever wanted to do, they didn't pursue it because of the criticism or lack of support they received early in their lives as illustrated by drunk Uncle Charlie's negative remark.

A 3 client I once worked with applied to a school to become a film editor. When she wasn't accepted into their program, she abandoned her film-editing dream and got a "regular" job. She woke up one morning with partial paralysis of her face and an inability to physically speak—she was otherwise healthy and in her 20s. Rather than apply to another college, she totally gave up her dream. This is a physical example of how emotions manifest in different aspects of the life of a 3—and how depressing your creativity can manifest physically and emotionally.

Depression

The 3 is often on an emotional roller-coaster, experiencing extreme highs and lows. If you're not using your talents, you'll experience mood swings. When you realize that your journey is an emotional one, you can learn how to manage the ups and downs more effectively. I don't know a 3 who hasn't experienced some level of depression in their lives. And often you can go from "awesome!" to "despair" in a moment (and back again).

This doesn't have to be a constant. When 3's learn to identify when they are literally and energetically *depressing* their emotions, their creativity, and their authenticity—then they can pass over into their true and joyful number 3 energy. The "flipside" for the 3 comes into play when you hold down (*depress*) your emotions and your creativity, the result is often a lingering depression that begins to define you. While many numerologists observe that the energy of the number 3 is the "pleasant path," I don't know one 3 who hasn't endured substantial emotional trauma. Your job is to blaze through it, find your joy and optimism, and model this for other people. Otherwise, the 3 can become a negative vortex—the depressive cynic or the person who lives only on a superficial realm. The 3 often lives with a certain sense of melancholy—underneath the buoyancy and humor can be a persistent sense of inexplicable sadness.

Superficiality

When a 3 is off track, one of the defaults is superficiality. The 3 can just skim the surface of life, stirring up emotional drama and trauma, feeling victimized, and placing all their energy into the surface elements of life. You can become slightly obsessed with your appearance, focusing on wardrobe, beauty products and procedures, and other aspects of your outward appearance to the point of distraction.

The 3 can be extremely impressionable. While this is part of the attraction of the 3 —enthusiasm, curiosity and openness— this can also become problematic when not held in check. The 3 can be the one who's always on the new diet, taking the new supplement, buying the latest whatever-it-is or ordering that piece of equipment they saw on the infomercial. While this isn't innately bad, the 3 can often become so impressionable that they focus the lion's share of their energy and resources on these sorts of things, much to the detriment of their over-all success or satisfaction.

The 3 can also default to always communicating through gossip. I once heard this observation: There are three levels of communication people can engage in. The highest form of communication revolves around ideas and problem solving. The second form of communication revolves around events. The lowest form of communication revolves around talking about other people. The 3 can resort to the lowest form of communication as a way of diverting from digging deeper within yourself.

Undisciplined Emotions

When you want your partner to support you as you wallow in unhealthy emotional expression, it won't work. This is often a way relationships disintegrate with a 3— when you expect your partner to become an emotional garbage pail as you wallow in negative or overly indulgent emotions. In this scenario, you're unwilling to work on positive solutions. Yet you expect your partner to listen and verify every fragment of your emotional rollercoaster.

You can become the ultimate procrastinator when feeling stuck or over-whelmed. The 3 has a tendency not to let go of past relationships. You mull them around in your head again and again, picking apart things said and done, what could've been and what wasn't, leveling blame on yourself and on others.

You tend to obsess over the smallest emotional hooks that bog you in a pool of cynicism or emotional defeat. Relationships can falter if depression becomes part of your daily existence.

You often find yourself grinding over an issue and shredding it into a pile of goo on the floor (so to speak). When this transpires, your best solution is just to leave it alone. Just stop. If it's really vital and needing your input, it'll come back into play for you when it's less emotionally charged.

The Glass is Half-Empty

When off-target, you're the anti-3. Instead of finding joy in life, you find despair. Instead of engaging with optimism, you're the ultimate pessimist. Instead of seeking fun, you think everything and everyone is stupid. When a 3 is way off, the glass isn't just half empty, the waiter never even came to the table with the water glass to begin with and it's everyone else's fault that the waiter ignored you. A 3 who presents in this manner hasn't been able to muster the courage or resolve to move through emotional blockages and extreme self-doubt. There's really nothing more grating than a 3 who refuses to embrace their birthright as a joyful, supportive, and emotionally communicative person.

START PUTTING IT TOGETHER

The way I'm presenting this information is somewhat unique to the way I have personally been able to deconstruct the Karmic Debt numbers—by getting a good grasp around not only the foundational number 4, but also to understand the characteristics of the number 3, which is where the trouble started last time! This is a way that I've developed my understanding about the nature of the Karmic Debt numbers through years of working with clients and investigating the repeating patterns that accompany each of the Karmic Debt numbers.

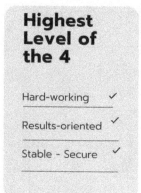

Karmic Debt 13/4

Abuse of RESPONSIBILITY & COMMUNICATION

Highest Level of the 4	Emphasis on the 3	Karmic Balance
Hard-working ✓	Performance ✓	Responsible yet flexible ✓
Results-oriented ✓	Emotional EQ ✓	Creative & communicative ✓
Stable - Secure ✓	Optimistic ✓	Stable & secure ✓

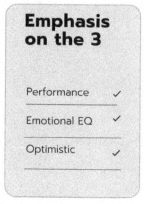

Here are some examples of some consistent challenges I see with people working with the 13/4:

- A tendency to hold on to negative experiences (usually having to do with romantic relationships or family) where they place themselves as the victim, despite the fact that their participation in the relationship dynamic was part of the problem.
- Difficulty committing to proper self-care—mostly physical exercise and diet.
- An inability to pursue the career or work that ignites their passion and then feeling angry that others don't offer them the type of opportunity they feel they deserve.

- Feeling continuous confusion about where to live, whether it's a certain type of house, apartment or geographical location.
- A constant feeling of exasperation and fatigue—feeling beleaguered and as though they're always getting the "short end of the stick."
- Just when the 13/4 has committed to something, they can impulsively abandon it and then feel stuck and confused about next steps—they want to skip the necessary steps.
- Having a very strong desire for someone else to take care of them (both emotionally and financially) and yet it rarely works out.

This is what I have experienced with the 13/4 when they're in the game and working with the most positive expression of the 13/4:

- Incredible drive and endurance to focus on a goal or task and bring it to fruition.
- Great sense of humor and ability to take the lead and get project accomplished. They trust their creativity and act on it pragmatically.
- Gifted at communication and often are artists, writers, presenters or teachers. They trust the process, are detail-driven, and aren't easily derailed.
- Focused on creating and maintaining good health routines and taking time to relax with meditation, gardening, time spent with animals or other activities that allow for true relaxation and down-time.

- Able to see their role in relationship dynamics and actively work on taking responsibility and using their words (and actions) to express thoughts, feelings, and opinions in a mindful way.
- They take the long-view while also living in the present moment as much as possible.
- Able to take things step-by-step while enjoying the journey along the way.
- They've learned not to take themselves—and other aspects of life—so seriously. The dynamic 13/4 has learned not to be offended or take things personally, particularly in work or job situations.

THE ULTIMATE MESSAGE

If you have the 13/4 in your numerology profile, I hope you're starting to see how the Karmic Debt shows up for you personally. Often, it's confusing because there's an arm-wrestle with a desire for the playfulness of the 3 and yet the 4 also demands that you buckle down and stabilize yourself.

The 3 (where you had trouble last time!) demands that you refine your levels of communication and bring a lighter spirit to everything you do. Yet the demands of the 4 are always at the control panel, putting you through tests of endurance and making sure you take responsibility for your thoughts, feelings, and actions.

I find people with the 13/4 have difficulty finding the lighter elements in life. Or alternately, find that settling in and planting their personal "root system" is next to impossible to achieve. Health concerns can often be part of the mix, with a demand to use self-discipline to eat well, get proper exercise, and to tune the mind with meditation and other brain-balancing practices.

Many 4s wrangle with ongoing (or on-and-off) health issues, often with a focus on lower back weakness, thyroid imbalances, food sensitivities, autoimmune and adrenal issues, and skin sensitivities.

And as if that isn't enough, you'll need to focus on your chosen task and not give up on it, no matter what kinds of obstacles cross your path. Fatigue and exhaustion are often the trademark of the 4—and the 13/4 is certainly no exception. While this might sound like "Ugh!", here's the ultimate message: *Your life's work is all about committing for the long-haul and the deep sense of satisfaction that will bring to you.*

The 4 is absolutely gifted at manifesting great things on every level, whether it's your organic garden, incredible photography or volunteer work. It can also show up as the building of a successful business, becoming an indispensable employee, devoted parent or famous celebrity. Where others would give up and throw in the towel, you carry forward, taking the necessary steps, dealing with the issues, and commandeering other people's personalities in order to get the job done.

The 13/4 who's balancing their *Karma* is the one who "whistles while you work." Often the work that speaks to the 13/4 has something to do with performance, communication, presenting, teaching/counseling, writing or other aspects that are key features of the calling of the number 3. So, if you have a Karmic Debt 13/4 in your numerology profile and you're attempting to decide how to focus your career and other aspects of your life, this Karmic Debt demands that you master the most positive and optimal aspects of the vibrant, expressive, and optimistic 3 while enveloping it into the fullest positive expression of the hard-working, systematic, and productive 4.

Usually, the qualities of the 3 and the 4 aren't on the same page. The 3's playful outlook can grate on the 4, while the 4's tendency to take everything so seriously and feel so "heavy" can baffle the pleasure-seeking and expressive 3. Yet with this Karmic Debt number, you have innate talents that connect with both the 4 *and the 3*—this is your *Karmic Gift!* There's an underlying driving force to use all that hard-working and pragmatic 4 energy to express, inspire, and motivate both yourself and others. Therefore, you can often feel a real sense of internal conflict or have a hard time managing the arm wrestle between two rather opposing forces. Learning how to integrate humor, emotional expression, and creativity into the more pragmatic and self-limiting 4 is the overall task.

While this might sound like *"What?"*—here's the ultimate message: Your life's work is all about committing for the long-haul. The 4 is absolutely gifted at manifesting great things on every level. With an emphasis on the 3, the 13/4 finds its niche when expressing through art, writing, presenting, teaching or any other form of positive expression. You're being asked to bring a playful and creative energy into everything you do. *Positive expression is mandatory!*

Working with a Karmic Debt number intensifies the issues relating to that number. It's not easy. It requires concerted effort and focused commitment. It's testing you and requiring that you rewire the way you work with communication, process, stability, knowledge, and hard work. The destructive path will feel more familiar since you've been there, done that. This time, you're being asked to extract yourself from riding in that same rut in the road—you're required to create a new way of working with these themes that have positive results for you and everyone around you.

A FEW WELL-KNOWN
13/4 LIFE PATH'S

Nicole Kidman   (June 20, 1967)
Oprah Winfrey   (January 29, 1965)
Grace VanderWaal (January 15, 2004)
Kate Hudson (April 19, 1979)
Octavia Spencer (May 25, 1972)
Nicki Minaj (December 8, 1982)
Drake (October 24, 1986)
Jimmy Fallon (September 19, 1974)
Brad Pitt (December 18, 1963)
Usher (October 14, 1978)
Bill Gates (October 28, 1955)
Elton John (March 25, 1947)
Jake Gyllenhaal (December 19, 1980)
Keanu Reeves (September 2, 1964)
Jordan Peele (February 21, 1979)
Shondra Rhimes (January 13, 1970)

ABOUT THE AUTHOR

**Felicia Bender, Ph.D. – The Prac-
tical Numerologist®** is the author of
*Redesign Your Life: Using Numerology
to Create the Wildly Optimal You*, *Master Numbers 11, 22, 33: The Ultimate
Guide* and *The Ultimate Guide To Practical Numerology: Mapping Your Path
& Purpose.* She earned a doctorate in
theater from the University of Mis-
souri–Columbia and is a certified in Pranic Healing™. Felicia is
passionate about writing, counseling, teaching, and presenting
ways to use numerology, spirituality, and intuition to understand ourselves and others on a deep level—to validate our life
purpose and to develop tools to understand how to trust our
own intuitive language. A frequent media contributor, she is
the resident numerologist for AstroStyle.com and you can find
her at FeliciaBender.com.

CPSIA information can be obtained
at www.ICGtesting.com
Printed in the USA
LVHW052108230423
745135LV00004B/689

9 780985 168230